Saumur and its château

On the road to the châteaux...

Hello! My name is Arthur and I'm 8 years old.
My sister's name is Louise. She is 11.

We were both born in Tours. Together, we will be showing you around the many treasures near where we live: the Loire Valley châteaux.

Off we go for a fun journey filled with surprises!

To make reading easier for you, difficult words have been ***highlighted in pink****, and are explained in the glossary p.63.*

There are so many treasures!

Here is a map of the châteaux we are going to visit.

As you will soon find out, each has its own history, style and original touch. A fascinating journey through the centuries. On our way, we will also come across lots of great historical figures. There will also be time for us to stop and explore a few curiosities and indulge in our regional specialities. Let's get going!

Background photo: Chaumont château

At the end of the Middle Ages,

during the 15th century, the kingdom of France had not yet been unified. **Several important lords, such as the Dukes of Burgundy, were against having Charles VI as king of France.** And there is more. At the time, *the Hundred Years War** was also going on, opposing France and England.

In 1418, the people of Burgundy - at the time faithful to the English - were occupying Paris. The future king Charles VII fled the capital. **He found refuge in the lands surrounding the Loire River,** that offered good protection against the enemy.

** The Hundred Years War actually lasted 116 years, from 1337 to 1453.*

In 1453, **peace returned to the country** (after France's victory), **but Charles VII enjoyed living in our neck of the woods and decided to stay.** The Loire Valley therefore became a favourite for the kings of France for many years.

The sovereigns would renovate the old Middle Age castles and build the most sumptuous abodes.
These brand new châteaux had to be able to welcome the entire **court** - meaning anyone close to the king (his ministers, advisers, servants, etc.). That could be up to 5,000 people!

This inspired more noble populations (Dukes, Marquis, etc.) - as well as ministers and officers in charge of the kingdom's accounts. In turn, they had wonderful châteaux built near the Loire River, boasting a new style: **THAT OF THE RENAISSANCE**. A new era was about to begin!

FORTIFIED CASTLES

They are typical of the Middle Ages. These castles are also known as **fortresses**. The sovereign used to live there with his family, soldiers and servants. Initially made of wood (and therefore particularly solid), then of stone, the architecture of this type of castle was decided on for a very special reason: to protect themselves against enemy attacks. Demonstration:

Nantes - The château of the Dukes of Brittany

THE MOATS: they go all around the building. They were a sort of large ditch that used to be filled with water. You can probably guess what they were used for: to prevent anyone from getting inside.

THE RAMPARTS: these high walls surrounded the castle. You could walk around the top of the ramparts to keep an eye on what was happening outside. This is known as **THE WALL WALK***.

THE DUNGEON: the highest tower in the castle. It used to serve as a lookout point, firing post and a last place to hide when the enemy had managed to enter the castle.

THE MACHICOLATIONS: important for ensuring the fortified castle's defence. They were stone balconies set right at the top of the towers. Their floors had holes in them, making it possible to watch for the enemy and throw projectiles at them.

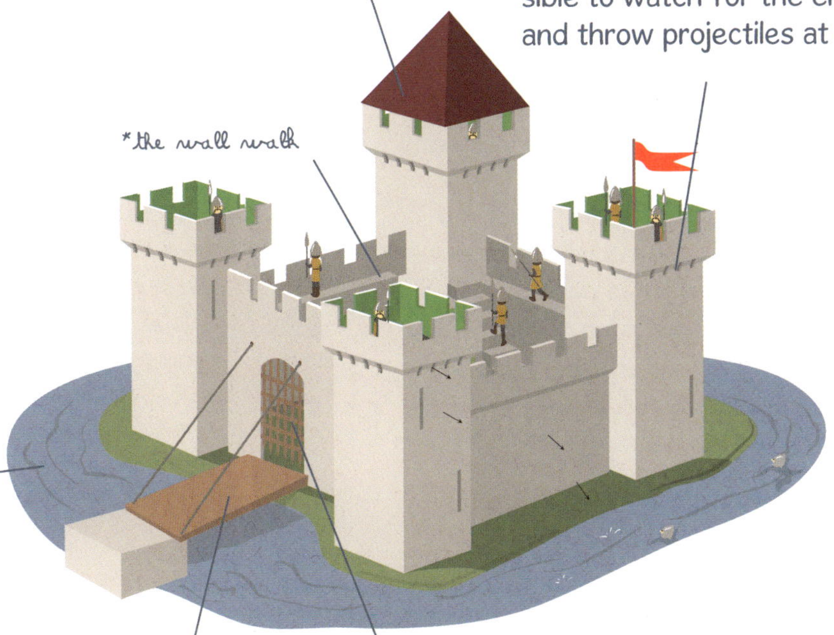

THE PORTCULLIS: this large iron gate was located right at the entrance. It could be lifted vertically to open and close.

THE DRAWBRIDGE: a wooden bridge hanging on chains. It was used to cross the moat when lowered.

THE RENAISSANCE CHÂTEAUX

With the arrival of the Renaissance era, fortified castles turned into châteaux. **They became pleasure homes that were lovely to live in.** Gone were the days of Middle Age fortresses. Nonetheless, the fortified castles were not destroyed. They were often transformed and made more beautiful.

From 1453 and the end of the Hundred Years War, peace returned to France. The country was almost entirely unified and entered an extremely prosperous era. **The fortified castles were no longer used as defence.** They became prestigious residences, richly decorated by painters and sculptors. Appearance was what mattered most. **Their style was inspired by Italian palaces** that kings Charles VIII, Louis XII and Francis I had discovered during their great wars against Italy.

Antiquity was back in style.

Italians considered that art at the time of the Greeks and Romans had never been equalled. For instance, they used it as inspiration in paintings, such as in The Birth of Venus *by Botticelli* *(see p. 12).* *In architecture, the famous Greek columns started reappearing.*

Doge's Palace in Venice

Here are the features specific to **RENAISSANCE CHÂTEAUX**.

The towers and wall walks were **covered with ROOFS**.

Very white and light-reflecting stone was used, known as **TUFFEAU**.
(see p.18)

Large façades **were built with big windows,** to let **THE LIGHT IN**.

Beautiful **STAIRCASES** were designed and built. The one in Chambord is quite simply magical!
(see p. 16)

Large **TAPESTRIES** were hung on the walls.

THE GARDENS became more decorative and extremely geometrical.

THE RENAISSANCE PERIOD

The Renaissance is an extremely important period of French and more generally European history. It was mostly set during the 15th and 16th centuries, so a very long time ago! It came just after the Middle Ages, and right before what is known as **modern times.**

It corresponds to a new-found literary, artistic and scientific approach.

The Renaissance first appeared in Italy during the 14th century, then came to France several years later. How? Thanks to our kings, and especially **Francis I.**

The Birth of Venus, by Sandro Botticelli, is one of the most famous paintings from the Italian Renaissance era.

At the time, they were waging wars against Italy. They fell under the country's charm, which they found much more refined and distinguished than the kingdom of France. They soon brought a new way of building, painting, thinking and playing music back to France with them.

Let's have a closer look!

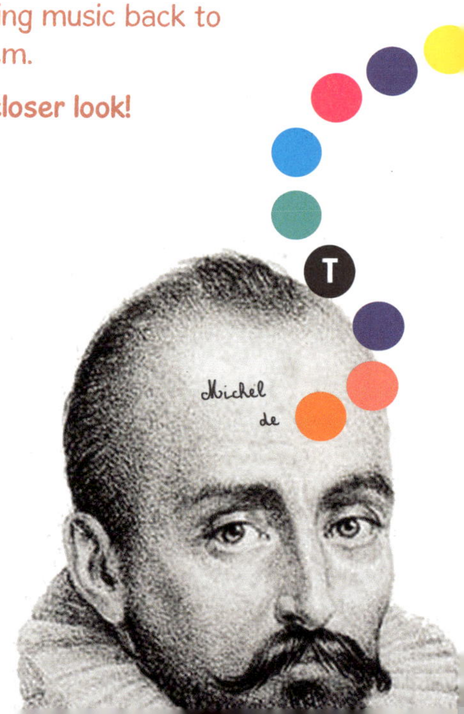

A NEW INTELLECTUAL WAVE

The Renaissance era brought on new ways of thinking, such as HUMANISM. It made mankind the heart of all our thoughts and put its trust in human nature.

The people belonging to this movement were known as humanists.
Among them were philosophers, authors and intellectuals.
Their goal was to improve humanity. In their eyes, knowledge was extremely important and was the key to progress, as well as to happiness!

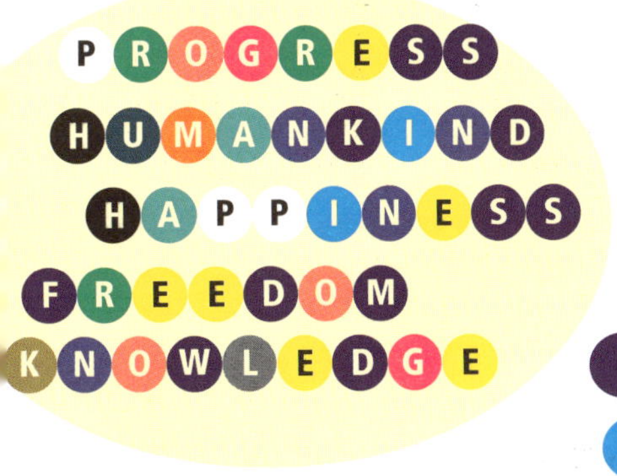

game

Find the name of these two leading 15th-century humanist authors by following the letter/colour code.

A NEW ARTISTIC WAVE

A revolutionary concept appeared in painting: PERSPECTIVE.

Artists started giving more depth to their paintings. The size of the people and objects painted grew smaller according to how far away they were. This made it feel closer to reality.

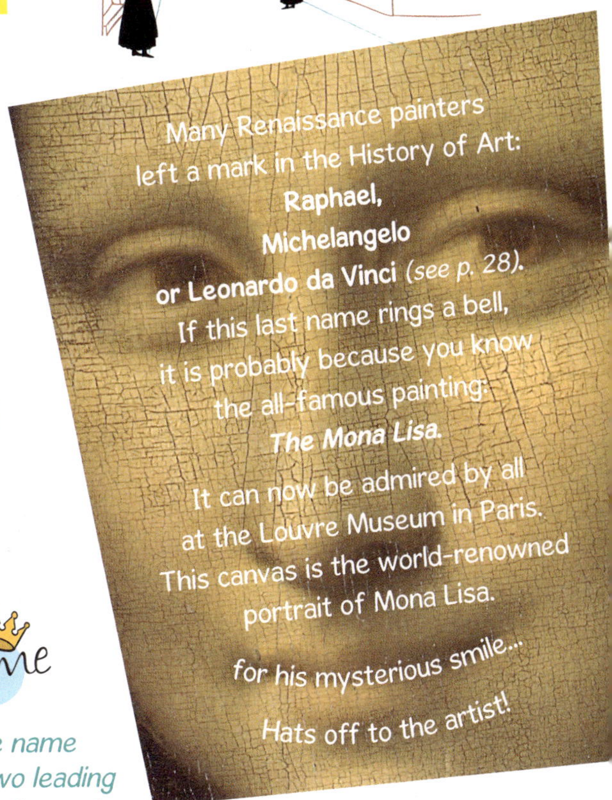

Many Renaissance painters left a mark in the History of Art: **Raphael, Michelangelo or Leonardo da Vinci** *(see p. 28).*
If this last name rings a bell, it is probably because you know the all-famous painting: ***The Mona Lisa.***
It can now be admired by all at the Louvre Museum in Paris.
This canvas is the world-renowned portrait of Mona Lisa.

for his mysterious smile...

Hats off to the artist!

The kings of France

who lived in the Loire Valley.

CHARLES VII
(1422–1461*)
married to Marie of Anjou.

LOUIS XI
(1461–1483)
married to Margaret Stuart then Charlotte of Savoy.

CHARLES VIII
(1483–1498)
married to Anne of Brittany.
No heirs.

Cousin of Charles VIII
LOUIS XII
(1498–1515)
married to Joan of France, Anne of Brittany and Mary Tudor.
No male heirs.

Cousin of Louis XII.
FRANCIS I
(1515–1547)
married Claude of France then Eleanor of Austria.

HENRY II
(1547–1559)
married Catherine de' Medici.

FRANCIS II
(1559–1560)
married Mary Stuart.
He died at the age of 16, with no heir.

Catherine de' Medici's second son
CHARLES IX
(1560–1574)
married Elisabeth of Austria.
No male heirs.

Catherine de' Medici's third son
HENRY III
(1574–1589)
married Louise of Lorraine.
No heirs.

HENRY IV
(1589–1610)
married Margaret of Valois (daughter of Catherine de' Medici and Henry II).

* years during which they reigned

FRANCIS I (1494-1547)

The great king of the Renaissance

He was very tall.
6'5" to be precise.
Quite impressive at the time.

Another original feature: **he came into power in 1515, aged only 21,** as the cousin and son-in-law of king Louis XII. Indeed, the latter died without having had a son, and therefore with no immediate successor.

Francis I had a long reign (32 years), which started with him triumphing over the Swiss in Marignan. The battle only lasted an afternoon and a night! As the leading royal knight, Francis I rode through the battle for 28 hours without any food or drink. He later fought other less glorious battles in Italy.

However, **this educated and curious sovereign made a huge discovery in this country: the Renaissance.**

He fell head over heels for it. Upon his return, he decided to give more importance to art, knowledge and science in France.

He also embellished or had built many châteaux. The most famous among them? Chambord, of course. (see following pages): his emblem was the salamander, and the F from Francis was sculpted everywhere.

Official language

As the absolute monarch, but also a modern king, Francis I also imposed French instead of Latin as the kingdom's official language.

With him in charge, the Middle Ages were nowhere to be seen in France.

CHAMBORD

The work of Francis I

Construction started: 1519

Francis I Louis XIV

220 tonnes of stone, **512** feet of façade, **426** rooms, **77** staircases and **282** fireplaces. This château is monumental. You will definitely be blown away by this Renaissance work of art, which we owe to Francis I.

In 1519, this young king - new to the throne and crazy about architecture - decided to build Chambord. He wanted it to exceed anything he had ever done. The château had to showcase how powerful France's royals were. This outrageous project kept up to 1,800 workers busy under his reign. It was only finished a century and a half later, thanks to Louis XIV. So Francis I never actually saw it completed. In fact, he stayed there a very short time: only 72 days!

Surprisingly, we still do not know the name of Chambord's architect.

However, many think that **Leonardo da Vinci's** plans may have been used to design this monument, which, with its central dungeon and large round turrets, looked somewhat like a medieval castle. Yet there is a definite touch of Italian style in the décor.

As for the park, it is practically as big as Paris: 5440 hectares!

As Francis I was so passionate about hunting, he had his château built in the heart of a forest filled with animals. Warthogs, stags, deer and game of all kinds still inhabit this vast domain.

You may even spot a few when driving into Chambord.

MOBILE FURNITURE!

For Francis I, Chambord was only a stop-over (often to go hunting). He would travel aroundfrom one château to the next. Along with his court (up to 5,000 people in total), he would carry all his furniture around with him. All his furniture could be disassembled (such as the beds). Practical, don't you think?
He never left anything behind. Not even the floorboards, which could be removed at the time.

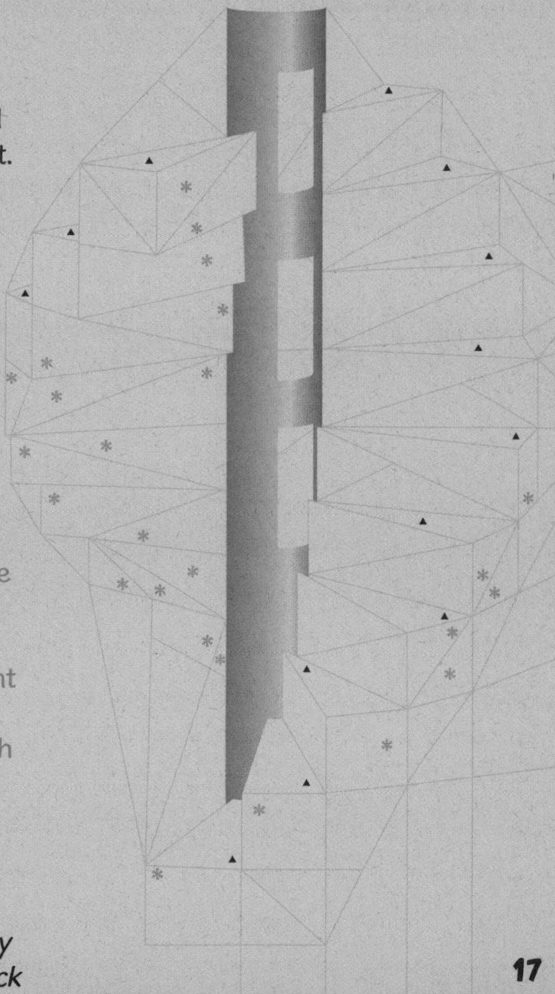

A MAGICAL STAIRCASE

Chambord's most amazing feature. In the middle of the dungeon, this "double spiral staircase" has two twin sets of stairs that wind around each other. If two people were to each use a different set of stairs, they could go up or down without ever crossing, but could spot each other through the small openings in the middle.

To see a pretty double spiral staircase appear, colour in:
*- the shapes containing * in grey*
- the shapes containing ▲ in black

TUFFEAU,
the stone of light

The château of Chambord

Tuffeau is a stone, and more specifically a limestone. That is what gives the châteaux and houses in the Loire Valley their beautiful creamy-white colour. When the sun is shining on the buildings, they look even more incredible. The creamy-white is then tinted with orange.
As early as the Middle Ages, **the region's cliffs would be exploited to extract the tuffeau,** a particularly soft stone that is much lighter than other varieties. **This makes it easy to handle and chisel.** Builders during the Renaissance period could work wonders with it. The best example? No doubt the château of Chambord. With its 512-foot façade, it proudly boasts a tuffeau-based construction.

game

Sculpt the lion's heard in the tuffea stone by tracing the right patterns with a black ball-point pen.

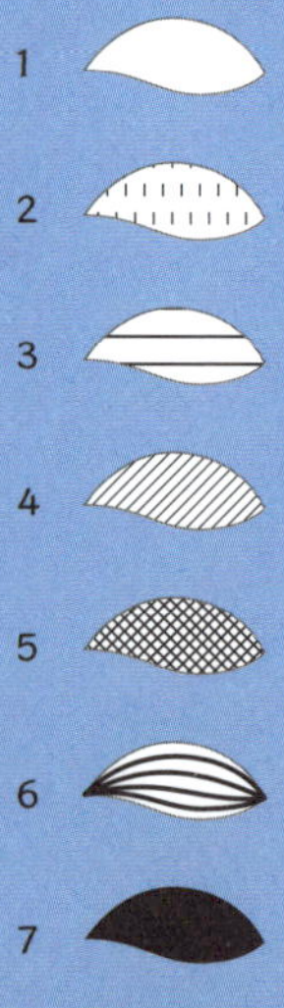

TROGLODYTES

What a funny word! Let's see what it means: a person who lives in a cave or home hollowed out in the rock.
Yes, by piercing the cliffs to extract the tuffeau stone, builders during the Renaissance era created several miles of underground galleries.
Local inhabitants actually settled down there.
Their homes were quite peculiar, no doubt about it. In any case, there was a major advantage to moving there: the temperature, which remained cool and unchanging all year long.

Abandoned from the 19th century onwards, **troglodyte houses came back into fashion in the 1980s** and were used again as mushroom farms, wine cellars and even luxury hotels!

Near Azay-le-Rideau, in Savonnières, Loches or Rochecorbon, there are many sites that will take you right into the heart of the stone.

game

To find out what the average temperature was in a troglodyte house, count the number of doors and windows on this façade.

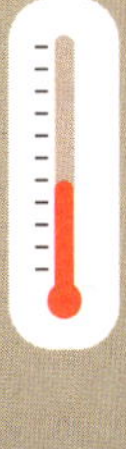

Between ☐ and ☐ °C,
all year round!

CHEVERNY

An inhabited château

Construction started: 1625

The Hurault fam

What in a barnacle's name do we have here? It looks like Captain Haddock's château. How right you are! Hergé drew his inspiration from the château of Cheverny when designing the Moulinsart château. He used the central part of the building, and got rid of the wings *(photo)*.

In the building right next to the château, the "Secrets of Moulinsart" exhibition delves us into the world of Tintin and his many comic books. From Professor Calculus' lab to Tintin's bedroom, it really feels like you're there with the characters! To be precise: it really feels like you're there with the characters!

But let's get back to the château's real story. Built during Louis XIII's reign, it has belonged to the same family for six centuries - the Hurault family - who still live in it.
As a result, this château is very lively and beautifully furnished. Among its many treasures: the beautiful Gobelins tapestry, or its impressive collection of weaponry and armoury.

As for its style, people say it is French architecture. Its structure - with its two wings framing a main body, aims for an **understated and symmetrical look.**
I know I could live there...

game

Talking about symmetry, do you know where to place a small mirror on the photo of the château so you can see it entirely?

The part of the château that inspired Hergé

WELCOME TO THE KENNELS

Cheverny's estate is home to about a hundred dogs, used for fox-hunting. This king of hunting - often on horseback - means fast animals are chased by a pack of dogs. It appeared around the same time horses were domesticated. At the time of Francis I, this kind of hunting became a real way of life, that greatly appealed to the French nobility. All the dogs can be seen in the château's kennels. You can even watch their morning feeding time at 11.30 am.

LET'S GO FOR A WALK IN THE PARK

Cheverny's estate also includes lovely gardens (vegetable garden, tulip garden, Apprentice's garden) and oceans' worth of lawns. A little further on, a charming park can be explored. Remarkable and very old trees (sequoias, cedars, lime trees) are dotted along the way. You can further your discovery on board a little electric boat, that travels down Cheverny's canal.

game *Which animal would you never see in the forest?*

BLOIS

Four châteaux in one!

Construction: 10th then 15th, 16th and 17th centuries

Louis XII

Francis I

Gaston, Duke of Orléans

France's sovereigns felt good in this château.
No fewer than ten queens and seven kings lived there.
Located right in the heart of the city of Blois, it provides a good overview of former architectural changes. Four periods, four styles, instantly noticed when entering the château's courtyard. Fascinating.

The counts of Blois. It all started with the counts of Blois. In the 10th century, they had a medieval castle built on the headland towering over the city. The **Estates General room** is practically the only one left from that period that can be visited.

Louis XII Born in Blois, Louis XII had his own palace built there from 1498. You won't have any problem recognising this wing, made of bricks and stone and adorned with lovely arches. They say the style is flamboyant Gothic.

Francis I 1515: Francis I had only just accessed the throne. He wasted no time and launched the construction of this château, inspired by Italian architecture. The ultimate form of Renaissance style: a façade with lots of windows to let the light in, and a magnificent stately spiral staircase so he could see and be seen by everyone.

Gaston, Duke of Orléans He would no doubt have loved to be king. As Louis XIII's brother, Gaston Duke of Orléans spent his whole life conspiring. He of course also wanted his own château, built from 1634. This château **was of a very classic style**, with its columns and pediments reminding us of **ancient Greece**.

"Mignonne, allons voir si la rose"

This is the most famous poem written by **Pierre de Ronsard**, born locally. With his beautiful rhymes, he wrote about a lovely young girl, Cassandre. He met her at a party held at the château in Blois. In this text, Ronsard pays tribute to Cassandre's beauty, yet warns her that it will not last eternally.

THE PORCUPINE

This large rodent was Louis XII's emblem. Its spikes symbolised **the royal defence** (protection against any attackers) and **offence** (its spikes could be launched onto the enemy like arrows). This was a way of showing how invulnerable the king's power was.

game

Louis XII's emblem has lost all its spikes. Can you add them back on with a fine-tipped pen?

MAGIC!

If you stop off in Blois, why not spice up your trip with a bit of magic? **The *Maison de la Magie* (House of Magic)** will delve you into the extraordinary world of **Jean-Eugène Robert-Houdin.** Inside, spread out over more than 21,000 ft^2, visitors can explore the history of magic, create shadow puppets, try out the "hallucinoscope" and of course discover the works of Jean-Eugène Robert-Houdin.

But who was this man? Born in Blois in 1805, Robert-Houdin was considered as the "father of modern magic". This fabulous illusionist opened a theatre in Paris entirely dedicated to magic.

Yet he was in no way predestined for this life as a magician. Initially fascinated with mechanics, he started out as a remarkable clockmaker. Only after having by chance opened a book on fun science and magic did he start devoting his life to this activity and revealing his talent.

HYPNOTISED...

1. Find a volunteer who agrees to be hypnotised for a few minutes.
2. Tell them to join their hands together and cross their fingers.

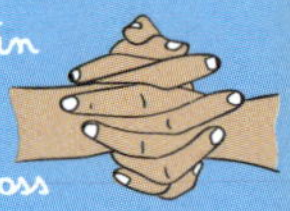

3. Swing a piece of jewellery in front of his/her eyes and ask him/her to follow it carefully...
4. Now ask them to raise their two index fingers, leaving the others crossed.

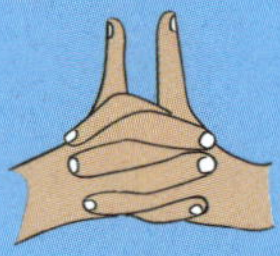

5. Explain to your audience that, thanks to hypnosis, you have magnetised your friend's index fingers. And, as if by magic, his/her index fingers will be drawn to each other!

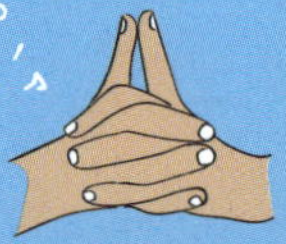

CHAUMONT-SUR-LOIRE

On the outside, we have a real fortified castle with its turrets, wall walk and drawbridge. Inside, the wings surrounding the courtyard clearly show a Renaissance influence. We owe these wings to Charles II of Amboise who had them built in the early 16th century.

This charming château is known to have welcomed two famous rivals: **Henry II's wife and mistress**, so both **Catherine de' Medici** and **Diane of Poitiers**. The queen bought the château of Chaumont in 1550. Nine years later, following Henry II's death, she made Diane of Poitiers exchange it against the château of **Chenonceau** which the king had given his mistress *(see p. 30)*. What a story...

In the 19th century, the prince and princess of Broglie restored the château beautifully. They also added luxurious stables and a wonderful landscaped park.

Since 1992, the park is home to the **INTERNATIONAL GARDEN FESTIVAL**. *From May to October, about thirty artists from all over the world are asked to design gardens according to a specific theme. Your turn!*

THEME: *A magical garden*

AMBOISE

The royal nursery

Construction started: 1492

Charles VIII was born there, Francis I grew up there and Henry II's children were raised there. The château of Amboise was well and truly a royal nursery. In the 15th and 16th centuries, it was **the favourite place to live for all of France's sovereigns.**

No wonder! Overlooking the Loire River from its rocky headland, it offers a panoramic view over the river and used to be the perfect observation post. **Most importantly, it was the first French château to be inspired by the Italian Renaissance style.**

In fact, it was upon returning from Italy that Charles VIII decided to pursue the transformation of Amboise's old fortified castle into a magnificent palace.
To do so, **he had Italian artists come over to France:** sculptors, architects, carpenters and gardeners.

Following his death in 1498, his successors - Louis XII and Francis I - carried on with the work and made the château the beauty it is today.

SO SILLY

King Charles VIII died at the young age of 28, after hitting his head against the lintel above a door in his château.

MINIMES TOWER

This tower was in fact an entrance gate used by knights and carriages to reach the château's terraces from the lower part of the town. **Horses could easily climb up the tower thanks to a spiral ramp with a very gentle slope.** It was in fact very similar to our current underground car parks.

From the top of the Minimes tower, you can look out over the Loire at a height of 130 ft.

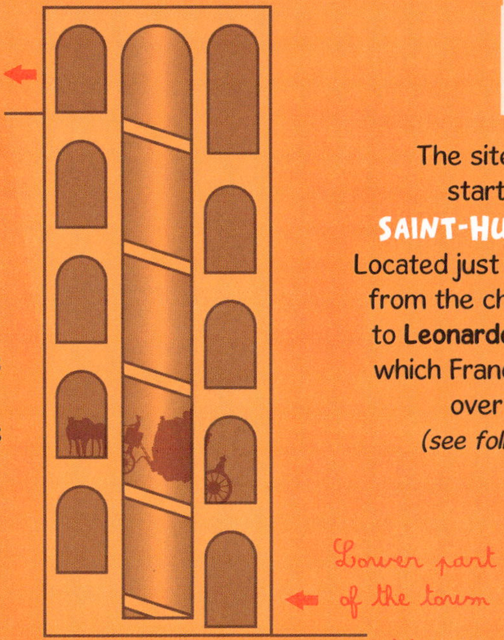

The site tour usually starts with the **SAINT-HUBERT CHAPEL.** Located just a few steps away from the château, it is home to **Leonardo da Vinci's tomb** which Francis I had brought over to France *(see following pages)*.

game

Find the 7 abnormalities on this carriage.

LEONARDO DA VINCI
(1452-1519)
Portrait of a genius

Painter, sculptor, engineer, scientist, inventor, architect. Leonardo da Vinci's curriculum vitæ (CV) is rather full. You probably know about his famous painting, the *Mona Lisa*. It is one of the most renowned paintings in the world. **Yet what this artist from Vinci - in Italy (hence his name) - loved above all else was inventing things.** Nothing could stop him. He loved trying to understand our universe and was passionate about everything. Indeed, it is because of his curiosity and careful attention to nature that we consider him now as such a genius.

We now know a lot of things about Leonardo da Vinci thanks to his countless notes and drawings, often displayed in museums. Some are plans of incredible inventions, that were impossible to build in his day. Only long after his death did we understand that he had come up with the idea of the helicopter, the diving suit, the machine gun, and even a forefather of the robot. Hats off to him!

game

This sketch by Leonardo da Vinci inspired one of the inventions on the right-hand page. Which one?

Did you know that Leonardo da Vinci wrote upside down to protect his inventions? How clever...

CLOS LUCÉ
CHÂTEAU

In 1516, king Francis I invited Leonardo da Vinci to France. He stayed in the Clos Lucé château, just a stone's throw away from Amboise. **He lived there for the last three years of his life, working on architectural plans for the king of France.**

Ateliers de Léonard de Vinci © Léonard de Serres

After discovering his bedroom, the Leonardo da Vinci **live model workshops** are a must. Perfectly recreated, they allow you to follow a creative day in the life of this giant artist. The rooms of the basement are also fascinating. They are home to many models of his inventions. In the *Leonardo da Vinci* park, you can even experiment with his life-size creations (military tank, swing bridge, paddle steamer).

CHENONCEAU
The Ladies' château

Construction started: 1513

Catherine Briçonnet 

Catherine de' Medici (married to king Henry II) 

Diane de Poitiers (mistress to...Henry II) 

With its sumptuous gallery that crosses over the Cher river, Chenonceau is a real gem. A sort of château-bridge that is unique throughout the world.

It was nicknamed the "Ladies' château", as its history is so intricately linked to women. Indeed, Chenonceau was imagined by Catherine Briçonnet (a noblewoman from Tours), then successively embellished by **Diane of Poitiers** (Henry II's mistress, to whom he gave the château as a gift) and Catherine de' Medici (Henry II's wife).

Catherine Briçonnet designed the current monument to replace an old fortified castle. She had it knocked down and only kept the dungeon, *known as the Marques Tower.*

We owe the famous bridge over the Cher River and lovely gardens to **Diane of Poitiers**. Catherine de' Medici, originally from Italy, adorned the bridge with two remarkable galleries, built one on top of the other, where she would organise huge parties. *Bravissimo!*
The two women were, of course, eternal rivals. Both of their bedrooms can be visited.

A CHÂTEAU FULL OF LIFE

With its huge fireplace in the Guards' room to warm you up in the winter, its beautifully furnished rooms and the many flower arrangements everywhere, Chenonceau could almost fool you into thinking the royal court was still living there.

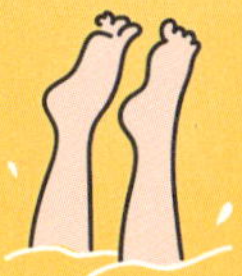

DIANE OF POITIERS' DAILY BATH

Henry II's mistress was a sporty woman (she rode every day) and took great care of her appearance and beauty by taking daily baths in the Cher River. Even when it was cold or raining. To get there, she would climb down a secret staircase in the kitchens.

game

When leaving the château, remember to stop off in the garden's maze. Made up of 2,000 yews each measuring just over 4 feet, it used to be the perfect place to relax and have a stroll. In this representation of it, find the path to the centre without frightening any of the rabbits.

THE LOIRE, A ROYAL RIVER

In the end, the river is the real star of our region. Indeed, we call them the Loire Valley châteaux. As you now know, many of them were built near the river as it was a fantastic way of blocking off the enemy.

But there is more. Right up until the railway was created in the 19th century, the Loire was also **the main means of transporting goods** from the inner part of the country to the sea. And vice-versa. Going one way, people would send off products to be sold: wine, cereal, metals, etc. Coming the other way would be salt or sugar and spices from the West Indies.

Lastly, you should know that the Loire runs for 629 miles and is therefore **the longest river in France. It is also registered as a Unesco world heritage site.**

game *Learn about and place the products in the grid that could be transported on the Loire during the 19th century.*

3
HAY
4
SALT
SILK
HEMP
5
SLATE
GRAIN
STONE
6
KNIVES
SHEETS
FRUITS
SPICES
WALNUT
WICKER
7
ORANGES
9
CHESTNUTS
FREESTONE

UNESCO

UNITED NATIONS EDUCATIONAL, SCIENTIFIC AND CULTURAL ORGANISATION.

Though it has a complicated name, this organisation is extremely important.

It helps children from all over the world **gain access to proper education.** Unesco is also tasked with **developing culture and science**, especially in poor countries. They rightfully consider that the better people are educated and taught, the less they want to fight others in wars. **Encouraging peace** is therefore a major goal set by Unesco.

Lastly, this organisation helps **promote and preserve our planet's exceptional sites.** To do so, it drew up a list that now counts **more than 1,000 sites.** Such wonderful treasures! In France, for example, the Mont-Saint-Michel, the Château de Versailles and **the Loire Valley with its many châteaux** are all registered on this list.

VALENÇAY
Talleyrand Prince château

Construction started: 1518

Charles-Maurice de Talleyrand (minister under Napoleon)

In 1803, **Charles-Maurice de Talleyrand-Périgord**, minister of Foreign Affairs under Napoleon Bonaparte, bought the château of Valençay. Actually, it was the Emperor's idea. He wanted his minister to have a sumptuous estate to host and impress world sovereigns.

Talleyrand was a subtle diplomat, often contested for his actions (he always found a way to stay in power), and was also a collector. He loved art and other things of beauty. Result: still today, the château's rooms are richly decorated with exceptional furniture, paintings and rare objects purchased by Talleyrand.

But let us not forget that when he came to own the estate, the château already had a heavy past. As a former fortress, **its construction was carried on in the Renaissance style throughout the 16th century by the rich Estampes family.** Inspired by Chambord, both the château and its surrounding park are huge.

SAY CHEESE!

Valençay is also the name of one of the region's most famous goat cheeses. At first, it was the shape of a tall, thin pyramid. Legend has it that Talleyrand decided to cut the top off the cheese before giving some to Napoleon. He was afraid its appearance would remind the Emperor of his defeat in Egypt, a country well-known for its...pyramids. Hence the cut-off shape of Valençay cheese.

THE CHÂTEAU'S SMALL THEATRE

Another one of Napoleon's ideas. To impress and entertain the Spanish royal family during their long (and forced) stay in Valençay, he suggested that Talleyrand have a theatre built within the château's outhouses. The theatre is truly splendid! It feels like nothing has changed since its inauguration in 1810. It can only be discovered during guided tours or as part of the **Talleyrand Festival**, organised yearly and dedicated to music.

game *Find the 7 differences.*

LOCHES
The royal city

No doubt about it, here we are back in the Middle Ages. **In year 1000 to be precise.** At that time, the count of Anjou Foulques Nerra had a formidable dungeon erected, towering 118 feet high. With its adjoining towers - Louis XI and Martelet - it also grew famous because of its terrifying cells.
What is there to visit? The Question room: a torture room aiming to make the accused confess. A little further on, the Graffiti room. As stated in its name, the walls are covered in prisoners' writings.

If you cross to the other side of the medieval city, you will find the beautiful Royal Abode. **Anne of Brittany stayed there, and Agnès Sorel - king Charles VII's mistress - lived there. And this is in fact where Joan of Arc - after her victory against the French - put pressure on Charles VII to be crowned king of France in Reims.** That was a major part of French history.

game

These strange symbols were found on the wall of a dungeon cell. What message did the prisoner leave for the person who would one day take his place?

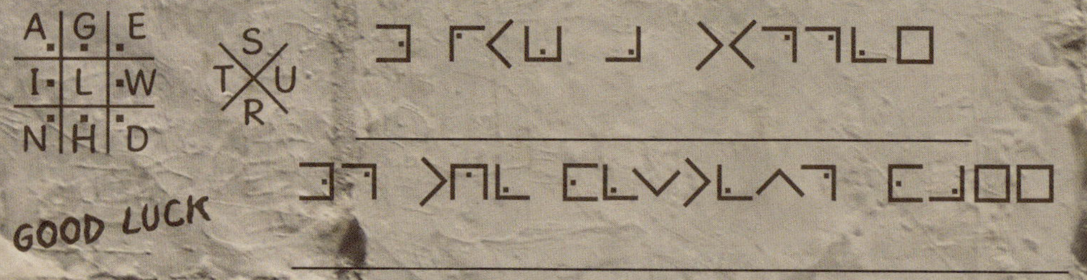

"LA BOULE DE FORT"

(Bowles)

This is a very strange game, that is still played a lot in the Loire Valley region. You play with balls, almost the same as when playing petanque. Except that the balls used are not perfectly round, and the playing field is not quite flat. In fact, the field is concave (forms a dip). Strange, isn't it? And there is more. This sport is often played...wearing slippers! These slippers are recommended to protect the alley, made of resin.

The rules are however simple: throw the balls as close as possible to the **"jack"** - a white ball placed on the playing field. The winning team is the first to score 10 points.

game

Which of these corresponds to Louise's throw?

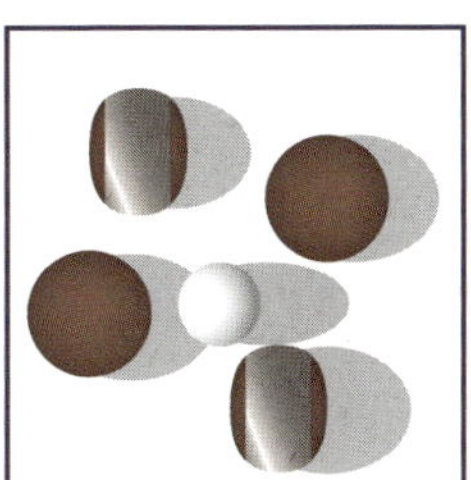

A

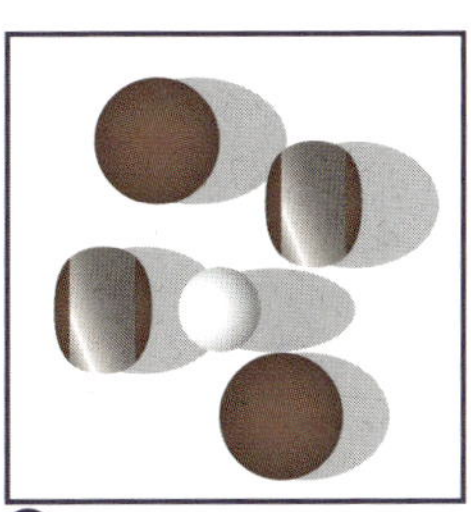

B

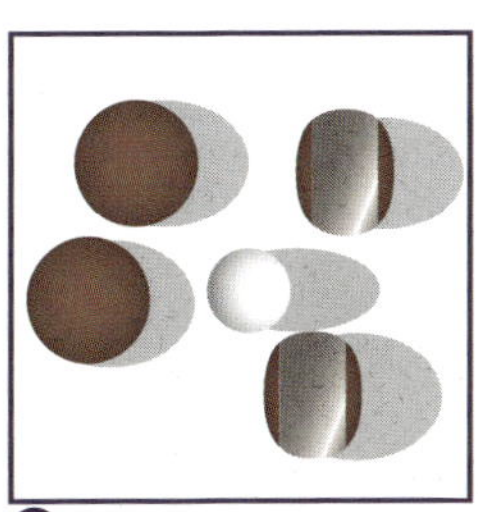

C

Francis I's salamander is sculpted more than 300 times on the ceilings and walls in Chambord!

LOUISE'S TOP TIPS

Look up:
the rose window in the Saint-Gatien cathedral is quite simply magnificent.
And there is nothing more beautiful than watching the sun set over the Loire in Tours.

Château of **SULLY-SUR-LOIRE**

The petrifying Savonnières grottos

Walks in the forest in the Sologne area.

My favourite thing to do: riding along the Loire on my bike.

On the way, we get amazing views of the river and châteaux. The perfect cycling path!

SMALL CHÂTEAUX

I love the Loire Valley's small châteaux. I feel good there. The one in Troussay is one of the smallest. You can even sleep there.

Château of **TROUSSAY**

TOURS

Welcome to our city! Obviously, it is perfectly located to go out and discover the Loire Valley châteaux. But Tours in itself is also worth a tour. For starters, you should know that **for a certain time during the reign of Louis XI, it was the capital of the kingdom of France.** Yes, seriously!

Things to see during your visit: the old town. In *Place Plumereau* (we call it "*Place Plume*"), you will see some pretty half-timbered houses that are all extremely old - they date back to the 15th century actually. Such a pretty area for having a hot chocolate out on a café terrace.

Our tour carries on to a historical monument: **Saint-Gatien cathedral** (Saint-Gatien was the first bishop of Tours). Its construction started in 1170 and took four centuries to finish!

Staircase wrapped around a bottle, reception area designed by an expert stonemason.

game

Match these wooden pieces two by two according to their shape. One match is not possible. Which one?

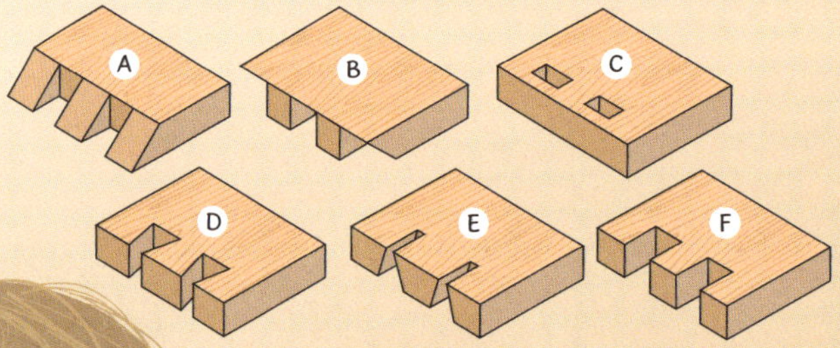

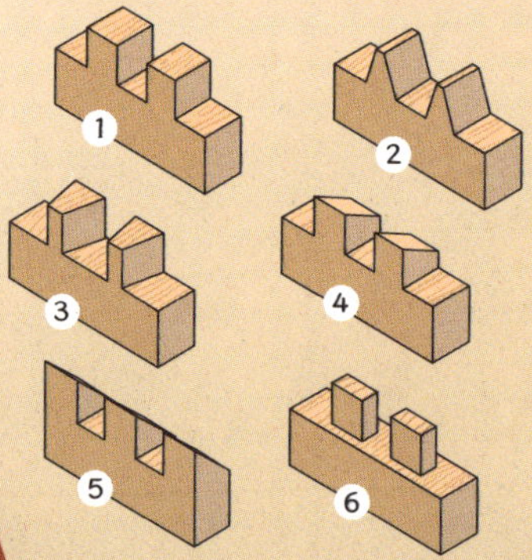

To finish off, a place we love to go: **THE MUSEUM OF EXPERT CRAFT WORKERS** ("*compagnonnage*"). It showcases all the trades that transform materials. For instance wood, stone, metal or even leather. There are lots of high-precision works: miniature roofs or an Eiffel Tower made of cut-up slate.

Photo by Richard Nourry/ Expert Craft Workers Museum in Tours

GASTRONOMY

The Loire Valley's local food is very tasty! There are lots of high-quality regional products, as well as delicious specialities!
Let's see what foods we can find!

Button mushrooms

In French, they are known as Paris mushrooms, but they do not come from Paris! They are actually grown near the Loire - close to Saumur and Tours. They can be found in the galleries dug up when exploiting the tuffeau stone. This stone maintains ideal humidity levels, perfect for growing mushrooms.

Goat's cheese

Another local speciality. There are three main ones, bearing the name of well-known towns:

Shortbread

Yummy - the Cher area is famous for its delicious crumbly shortbread biscuit! It is a local speciality. It is round and perfectly golden.

Rillettes/potted meats

Everyone in Tours loves them and they are a must-have speciality! Rillettes have existed for a long time: they were first created in the 15th century.

VILLANDRY
Extraordinary gardens

Construction started: 1532

Jean Le Breton

Joachim Carvallo

They are so beautiful, they almost make us forget there is a château to see too!

We owe these remarkable gardens to **Joachim Carvallo**, a Spanish scientist. In 1906, he bought the château of Villandry, which was about to be demolished! And he had an amazing idea in mind: **recreate the Renaissance gardens** that had been replaced with an English landscaped garden in the 19th century. Obviously, he had no photos of the previous gardens to get his inspiration from. So, being a scientist, he meticulously studied all the literary and archaeological clues he could find. Mission accomplished.

All you need to do is climb up to the belvedere to admire these beautiful French gardens: the decorative garden with its four squares forming **the love gardens, the water garden, the simples garden** where all the herbs are planted (thyme, mint, tarragon, etc.) and the amazing **vegetable garden** with its nine identical squares.

The Love Gardens

Tender love

Passionate love

Fickle love

Tragic love

THE CHÂTEAU

Villandry is the last of the major Renaissance châteaux, built along the Loire river banks. Its construction was overseen by **Jean Le Breton**, a minister under king Francis I.
As such, he had an old Middle Ages fortress destroyed, the remnants of which today include a single large turret.
The château distinguishes itself with its simplicity and well-established architectural ideal of the time: symmetry.

AN EXTREMELY DECORATIVE VEGETABLE GARDEN

In the vegetable garden's nine squares the geometric patterns are all different. Indeed, these squares have vegetables and flowers planted in them whose colours alternate: blue for the leeks, red for beetroot and green for lettuce. In the autumn, orange is the most visible colour because of the huge pumpkins.
In total, 40 varieties are planted in this multi-coloured patch, carefully cared for by the château's nine gardeners.

Can you help this gardener finish his design by colouring in using the right colours?

LANGEAIS

Delving back into the olden times

Construction started: 1465

Louis XI

Charles VIII and Anne of Brittany

If you arrive exactly when the château opens, you will be able to see the drawbridge drop down. Welcome! This is how things are in Langeais. It feels like we are back in the 15th century. You can even go completely around the wall walk. **It is completely covered and runs along a total of 426 feet. It really is one of a kind.** As you may have understood, this château is like a real medieval fortress. Yet contrary to what it seems, it served more as a residence than as a defence system.

game

B=A ; C=B...

Built by king Louis XI, it stands as a lovely example of how architecture was perceived at the end of the Middle Ages. On the courtyard side, the façade and its beautiful windows made it **an extremely pleasant place to live.** Inside, each room has its own large stone fireplace, and the chambers were all very refined.

Long forgotten after the 15th century, **the château was bought back at the end of the 19th century** by a businessman, Jacques Siegfried. He restored and furnished it entirely. What a great initiative!

Actually, **you should know that a first castle had been built here** by Foulques Nerra, count of Anjou, in 994 to contain the attacks against the counts of Blois. **Its dungeon is the oldest in France, and can still be admired today.**

A HISTORICAL WEDDING

In Langeais, on 6 December 1491, a secret yet memorable wedding took place: that of king **CHARLES VIII AND ANNE OF BRITTANY**.

This union led to **the duchy of Brittany being unified with the kingdom of France** *(see p. 60)*. In the château, fifteen life-size wax characters play out the event, complete with sounds and lights.

details of one of Langeais' tapestries

Richly furnished, the château of Langeais will take you back to how people lived in the Middle Ages. It also boasts a collection of tapestries from the 15th and 16th centuries. In fact, at the time, tapestries were part of the furniture. They would serve as insulation from the cold stone, block any draughts and decorate the rooms.

game

What colour is each bobbin of thread?

AZAY-LE-RIDEAU
A château on an island

Construction started: 1518

Gilles Berthelot (treasurer to the king) **and Philippe Lesbahy**

the Marquis of Biencourt

Truth be told, it does look very much like a medieval fortress.
Yet the château in Azay-le-Rideau is the perfect example of Renaissance style. Even though it was only completely finished in the 19th century.

It all started in about 1510. Gilles Berthelot, adviser to king Louis XII and treasurer of France, purchased a fortress (slightly in ruins) dating back to the Middle Ages.

He transformed and embellished it, with some help from his wife, Philippe Lesbahy. No, you did not read the wrong name: at the time, it was given both to women and men.

Then everything stopped in 1527. Gilles Berthelot, in charge of the kingdom's money, kept a little for himself. Afraid he would be caught and even executed, he preferred to flee - leaving his wife and château behind him.

Only in the 19th century, when the Marquis of Biencourt arrived, did the work pick up again and was finally completed.

Regardless, the final result is astounding.
Resting on an island in the middle of the Indre river, with its moats, turrets and machicolations, it definitely reminds us of... a fortified castle.
Except that all these items were designed and created with a great deal of refinement and elegance. So very charming!

MIRROR, MIRROR...

This château seems to care about its appearance. It is reflected in a mirror of water. This mirror is in fact an arm of the river that surrounds the château. In 1950, some work was done to widen this river arm. Result: the current was slowed down, the water was able to stabilise and the château can now admire itself. And so it should!

ROYAL PRESENCE

On the walls of the château, before climbing the Italian-style staircase, two funny little animals were sculpted:

The salamander - this legendary fire-spitting animal was Francis I's emblem.

The ermine represents his wife, Claude of France. Something for everyone.

game

Count all the mixed-up ermines and salamanders. Which of these animals is there the most of?

USSÉ

A fairytale castle

Construction started: 15TH century

André Le Nôtre

Marquis of Valentinay

It's true that with its lovely silhouette standing out among the trees, this château looks like it has just stepped out of a fairytale. It is easy to understand where the writer **Charles Perrault** got his inspiration to set the backdrop for the famous tale of **Sleeping Beauty**, published in 1697. In fact, in the heart of the dungeon, some scenography will depict the Wicked Fairy Godmother and Prince Charming.

The construction of Ussé only truly began in the 15th century. Its style transcended the ages. Initially designed as a fortified castle (look at its many turrets and battlements), it then took on a Renaissance style (façade at the back of the courtyard), followed by a more classic one during the 16th and 17th centuries, namely through the work done by the **Marquis of Valentinay**. Thanks to his large fortune, he turned it into a magnificent leisurely abode.

Nowadays, the château of Ussé is still a private residence, but it can still be visited. It belongs to the **Duke of Blacas** - his family have been guarding this enchanting place for the last 200 years.

VAUBAN AND LE NÔTRE

Two leading men from the 17th century made the château of Ussé the beauty it is today.

The Marquis of Vauban, master of the fortifications, imagined a terrace just above the gardens. French-style gardens designed by **André Le Nôtre,** king Louis XIV's gardener, to whom we owe the park surrounding the Château of Versailles...that's right!

INSPIRATION

The Loire Valley has always been a feel-good place. Renowned writer and philosophers would come to Ussé to see just how sweet life could be: **Charles Perrault, Jean de la Fontaine, Voltaire** and even **Chateaubriand** who wrote part of his memoirs there.

game

WORDSEARCH

Cross out all five of Charles Perrault's tales, hidden away in the grid.

You can read the words in all directions (except diagonally), and use the letters several times.

N	I	C	R	N	B	O	O	I
D	R	D	C	I	S	K	T	T
E	A	Y	B	O	S	F	S	H
R	E	L	L	A	U	P	M	U
G	B	E	U	K	I	N	B	T
N	I	A	H	S	E	D	L	T
E	P	U	T	Y	U	O	I	N
E	L	S	F	E	K	N	T	G

BLUEBEARD
CINDERELLA
PUSS IN BOOTS
DONKEYSKIN
THUMBLING
SLEEPING BEAUTY

The remaining letters will form the title of the illustrated tale.

ROYAL FASHION

Clothes during the Renaissance period

As you can probably imagine, noble folk living in the Loire Valley châteaux did not rule in jeans and tennis shoes!

Fashion did however grow slightly freer during the Renaissance era: clothes became more decorative, elegant and representative of social status. Embroidery came into style, as did thick and therefore expensive materials, jewellery and lace... How lovely!

Several types of clothes became important at that time.

SHIRTS:
wearing a shirt was a sign of power and wealth! It was important for noble populations to show off their nice white shirts.

Louis XII, king of France (p. 14)

Marie de' Medici, queen of France

Draw a pretty ruff on the unfinished portrait of Marie de' Medici.

RUFFS

No one wears them anymore, but they used to be all the rage! It was a pleated and fairly bulky collar. **It would be worn by both men and women.** Their neck would look rather funny in it!

FARTHINGALE HOOPS

An extremely important accessory invented in the 16th century. It is a sort of underskirt made of material, and wood or iron to give the dress its large volume.

game

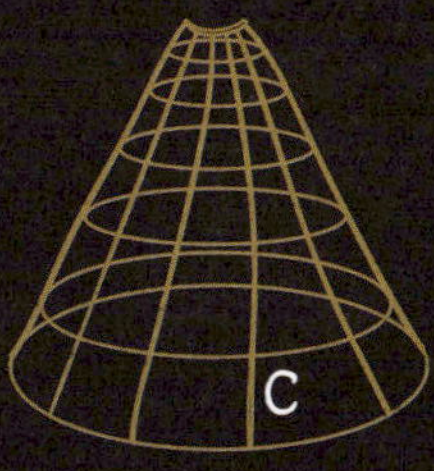

Match the right farthingale accessory with each model.

SLEEVES

At the time, people owned several pairs of sleeves! It was very easy to change them according to you mood and what you felt like wearing. A single dress could have about ten different pairs of sleeves. How original!

In fact, a famous French expression says "**that's not a pair of sleeves**". It is used when talking about something that is not easy to do, in reference to changing a pair of sleeves which used to be so simple!

CHINON

When discovering the Loire Valley châteaux, the best would be to start with the royal fortress of Chinon. It sheds a lot of light on surrounding historical facts. Here is a summary of important events.

10TH CENTURY
THE COUNTS OF BLOIS THEN THE COUNTS OF ANJOU

Up on their rocky headland, the Counts of Blois began the construction of the fortress. They were looking to protect themselves against their neighbouring enemies, the Counts of Anjou. In the end, in 1044, the latter seized power in Chinon.

12TH CENTURY
HENRY II PLANTAGENET RULED BASED IN CHINON

Henry II Plantagenet was Count of Anjou. In 1154, he became king of England. Shortly before that, he married Eleanor of Aquitaine and therefore ruled over **a huge part of the territory - from England to the Aquitaine area. Chinon became the centre of his possessions.** He had a palace erected there - Saint-Georges fort

LATE 12TH - EARLY 13TH CENTURY
CHINON WAS ATTACHED TO THE KINGDOM OF FRANCE

Upon Henry II's death, his sons Richard Lionheart then John Lackland took over from him. They were opposed to the king of France, Philip Augustus, who wanted to take back their territories. In 1205, **Philip Augustus seized the fortress of Chinon.** The town was thus attached to the kingdom of France.

1429
A HISTORICAL ENCOUNTER

It was the Hundred Years' War. Threatened by the English, king Charles VII drew back into his land in the Loire Valley. He turned Chinon into one of his residences. **It was here, in February 1429, that Joan of Arc came to meet Charles VII.** She managed to convince him to entrust her with an army to fight the English in Orléans. She freed the town on 8 May!

WINES
FROM THE LOIRE VALLEY

A big thanks to the Romans! That's right, when they occupied Gaul, our invaders left their wine-growing culture behind for us to savour. Right up to the Loire Valley. **2,000 years later, our region's wine-making is still going strong.** You obviously do not drink wine, but the vineyards offer breathtaking views. To best enjoy them, you could drive along the wine route, that snakes through the countryside for several dozen miles. It is the longest in France.

The most well-known of all Loire Valley wines is certainly the one made in Chinon. The renown is partly due to the great French writer, **François Rabelais** (1494-1553). He often talks about it in his novel *Gargantua*.

game

This object was invented by the Gauls. Still today, it is used to mature wine.

Mister **RABELAIS**

Let us now go and meet a famous writer and humanist *(see p. 9)*: François Rabelais.

Born near Chinon in the 15th century, this extremely learned man also practised medicine. Most importantly, he was the one to write the tales of two very special characters, **Pantagruel and Gargantua.**
These two giants only ever had one thing in mind: eating and drinking! Their adventures are really very funny.

Rabelais was also one of the first to use **spoonerisms**.
The principle is quite simple: by switching a sentence's letters or syllables around, you can create a completely different meaning*.
It is very funny and gives Rabelais' novels an original touch.
Indeed, he wanted to reach out to a wider audience and make them want to read and learn. He considered that making his readers laugh was a good way to draw their attention!

** « Rindercella slopped her dripper » instead of « Cinderella dropped her slipper »*

game

When he was a baby, the giant Pantagruel drank the milk of:

☐ ☐ ☐ ☐ *cows!*

Count the number of cows and multiply that by one hundred!

SAUMUR

You can see its pretty silhouette towering proudly over the Loire. The château in Saumur has a long history.

It starts in the **10th century** with the Count of Blois, Theobald I, who had the château's first fortifications built.

Then, just like in Chinon *(see p. 52)*, the Counts of Anjou seized it.

Once returned to the kingdom of France in 1203, its construction was pursued thanks to Louis IX who turned it into a real fortress.

His work was continued by Louis I of Anjou who made a stunning residence out of it. The round turrets were replaced with octagonal towers and the roof was covered in slate.

From the 17th century onwards, the **château was used as a prison,** saving it from destruction.

Finally, **the city of Saumur** bought it back in 1906 and restored it magnificently.

THE CITY OF HORSES

Nowadays, the château is home to an original museum dedicated to horses! You can see lots of spurs, saddles, stirrups and other horse-riding accessories used at the time of the kings.

Saumur is also home to a famous **cavalry school: THE "CADRE NOIR".** Since 1815, the best riders **in the country have been trained there.** Horse-riding is a real art here!

game *One of the outlines appears twice. Which one?*

The abbey of FONTEVRAUD

This place is really intriguing. Fontevraud abbey was founded in 1101, **and is the biggest in Europe.**

Monks and nuns would work and live here, in silence. Original touch: for close to two centuries, it was managed solely by women. **The abbesses** (high-ranked nuns) **had all the power**. Even over the men.

Right in the middle of the Abbey's impressive church, **do not miss out on the recumbent statues of Henry II Plantagenet** and his wife **Eleanor of Aquitaine** *(see p. 52).*

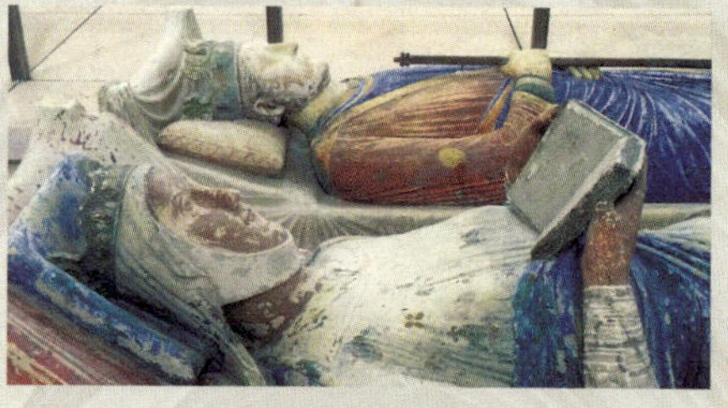

***Recumbent statues** are sculptures representing the deceased people lying down. They are usually placed on top on their graves.*

Eleanor of Aquitaine, both rich and devout, had made many donations to help with the abbey's development.

SUCH A SAD FATE!

In 1792, after the Revolution, Fontevraud was turned into **a prison**, until it shut down in 1963.

A time for DISCOVERIES

The Renaissance period was dotted with inventions and discoveries that changed the world.

Here is a brief overview.

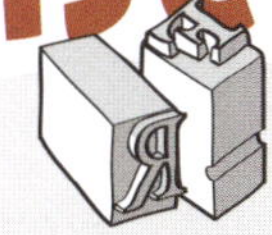

PRINTING

Towards 1450, in Germany, **JOH◆NNES G●★ENBERG** invented characters (letters, signs) embossed in lead, that could be moved around easily. This was the start of **★YPOGR◆PHY**. This process made it possible to print books in lots of copies.

This revolution encouraged the **★R◆NSMISSION OF KNOWLEDGE** and most importantly **the ideas** put into writing by **H●M◆NIS★S** *(see p. 13)*.

MAJOR DISCOVERIES

Up until the 14th century, seamen never sailed too far from the coastline as they had no real landmarks and their ships were not sturdy enough.

Once the **COMP◆SS** and **◆S★ROL◆BE** had been invented, Europeans started sailing much greater distances. Also, at about the same time, a safer and quicker boat was designed: the **C◆R◆VEL**.

This marked the beginning of many new adventures!

- In 1492, **Christopher Columbus** discovered **◆MERIC◆**.
- In 1498, a Portuguese man named **Vasco de Gama** was the first European to reach India by boat.

ASTRONOMY

In the middle of the 16th century, the Polish astronomer **Nicolaus Copernicus** was the first to understand that the **S●N** was in the **CEN★RE** of the **●NIVERSE** and that the **E◆R★H ★●RNS ◆R●●ND** it.

Before we used to think the Earth was the centre of the universe. This theory was confirmed a little later on by a scientist named **Galileo.**

game

Did you find which letters matched these symbols?

● ___ ★ ___ ◆ ___

ANGERS
A fortified castle in the city

Construction started: **TOWARDS 1230**

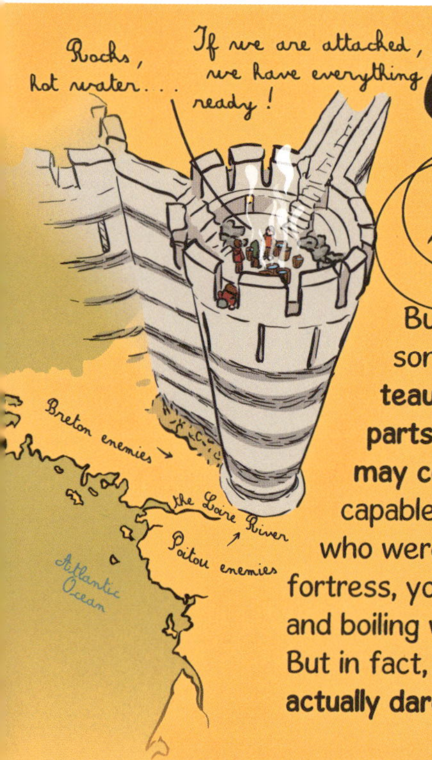

What a giant this château is! Especially as you do not expect to find such a huge fortress right in the heart of the city.

Built by order of Blanche of Castile and her young son Louis IX (future Saint Louis) from 1230, **this château is extremely imposing with its impenetrable ramparts and 17 watch towers able to resist any attack that may come their way.** A real fortified castle at the time capable of pushing back any Breton or Poitou enemies, who were close to the king of England. From the top of this fortress, you could throw rocks and boiling water on attackers. But in fact, **no enemies ever actually dared come close.**

In the 14th century, under the auspices of the Counts of Anjou and namely Louis I of Anjou, the castle became the most elegant château of the royal court, that people enjoyed staying in.
Later, towards 1432, René of Anjou (nicknamed "Good King René"), Count of Anjou, had the royal Abode built. **The château, with its remarkable gardens, was thus turned into a palace.**

The next part was not as pleasant: the fortress only just avoided being destroyed and, until 1856, was used as a prison.

HOW AMAZING!

Anger's château is home to a one-of-a-kind piece of art: **THE APOCALYPSE HANGING.**
Louis I, Duke of Anjou, had already launched the château's restoration process and ordered this giant woven tapestry **FROM 1375.**
It represents the **Apocalypse of Saint John*** and include many different drawings.
Originally, it measured **460 FEET** long. But over time, parts of it were lost.
Now, there is still **330 FEET** left, depicting more than **200 CHARACTERS.**
It is fun because it almost looks like a cartoon.
In any case, it is the longest and most ancient tapestry in the world!

game

Restore this extract from the hanging of the Apocalypse using the details below. Watch out, one of the pieces was not initially part of the tapestry!

** This tale, written by Saint John, is the last book of the Bible.*

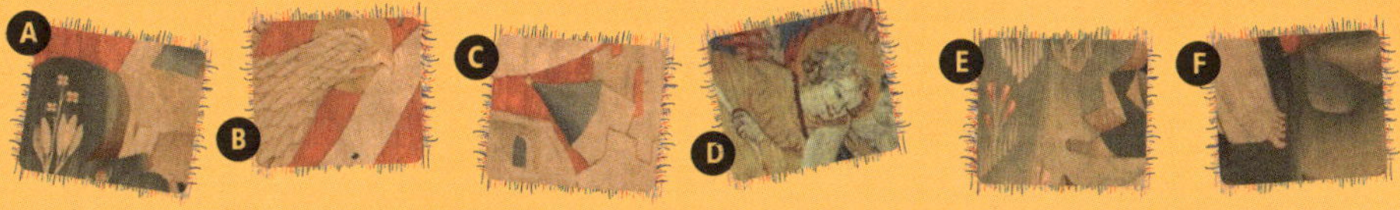

NANTES

The château of the Dukes of Brittany

Construction started: 1466

Anne of Brittany

Duke Francis II

Here we are, at the end of the 15th century. Brittany was not yet part of France. It was a **duchy**. Indeed, it was governed by **a Duke, Francis II.** Problem: the royal power wanted to include this region in the kingdom of France and began attacking it.

To protect himself, Francis II had a huge new fortified castle built in Nantes, Brittany's main town, on top on a former 13th-century one. He made the most of it and turned the castle into a palace that was pleasant to live in for the ducal court.

After his death in 1488, his daughter Anne became Duchess of Brittany at the tender age of 11! During her reign, she carried on with her father's major work and fought tirelessly to defend her duchy. Despite her best efforts, Brittany was annexed to France in 1532.

Having been entirely renovated in the 1990s and 2000s, the château of the Dukes of Brittany is now home to a fascinating museum telling us about Nantes' history.

game

Whoops! A few mistakes have slipped into the text below.
Can you replace them with the right ones in blue?

TOWN AND COURT

The Dukes' meadow stands out with its **two very different styles.**

Outside, a formidable big dress protected by deep coats, and defended by red hearts and seven large tool kits made of granite. In total, the wall walk runs for 1,600 feet.

Inside, the spook's elegant residence comes as a contrast to the white tuffeau bone. The funky dance style had just started to appear.

Dukes' fortress stone moats
Renaissance château large turrets ramparts

TWICE A QUEEN!

Anne of Brittany was only 15 when she married the king of France, Charles VIII, to ensure peace between the duchy of Brittany and the kingdom of France.

But Charles VIII died 5 years later. By contract, she was forced to marry his successor, Louis XII. **She was therefore crowned queen a second time.** She was the only person in French history to have experienced that.

AND FOR DESSERT...

TARTE TATIN

Have you heard of this famous pastry? This pie is quite original: it is made with caramelised apples, and served... upside down! **Did you know it came from the town of Lamotte-Beuvron, in the Loir-et-Cher area?** It was invented by two sisters, **Caroline and Stéphanie Tatin**. They held a local restaurant, and their dessert became famous because of a mistake they made. They had prepared an apple tart, but forgot the pastry on the bottom... So they added it later, on top of the caramelised apples. When the time came to serve the dessert, they dropped it and it turned over onto a plate. People have been crazy about it ever since!

WHAT YOU WILL NEED FOR THIS RECIPE

10 apples
(that stay firm even when cooked)

120 g of sugar
90 g of butter

1 roll of puff pastry
(or shortcrust pastry)

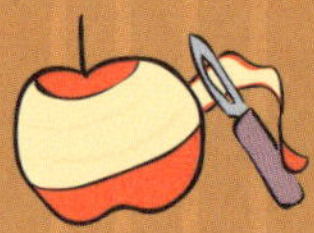

1
Peel the apples and cut them into quarters.

2
Put 40 g of butter and 50 g of sugar into a hot pan and cook the apples until they soften.

À faire avec un adulte

3
In a saucepan, melt 40 g of butter and 60 g of sugar with a little bit of water. Leave to cook until the mixture browns.

4
Pour the caramel into a greased mould. Sprinkle with sugar.

5 Arrange the cooled apples close together in the mould. Sprinkle with sugar and add the remaining butter.

6
Cover with the pastry and pinch the sides in well. Then cook in the oven heated to 200°C for 30 min.

7
Wait for the pie to cool completely before placing a large plate on it and flipping it over!

GLOSSARY

Half-timbered houses in Rennes

Absolute monarch:
A king with all possible powers.

Adjoining:
Next to or even touching a place.

Belvedere:
A place located right at the top of a building, a little like a terrace.

Curriculum vitæ (CV):
Document that introduces a person and their professional background.

Diplomat:
In politics, this person takes care of representing their country abroad.

Diving suit:
A special piece of clothing used to go underwater, breathe and work there.

Ducal:
Belonging to a duke or duchess.

English landscaped garden:
An English landscaped garden boasts irregular shapes. It differs from French-style gardens, whose shapes are much more geometric.

Expert Craft Work:
Training period during which a worker must become an expert, guided by a master. This kind of training is possible in trades focusing on manual labour and working with different materials. For instance, bakers are often expert workers.

Flamboyant Gothic:
Name of the last period of Gothic art. This form of architecture features a lot of curves and arches.

Fortifications:
Constructions (ramparts for instance) aiming to defend against the enemy.

Game:
Animals that are hunted to be eaten.

Gobelins (tapestries):
Tapestries made with richly illustrated materials. More specifically, they are tapestries woven by the French Gobelins Manufacture. The latter was created in 1601, thanks to Henry IV.

Half-timbered:
Half-timbered houses are made with wooden beams and light materials such as plaster or cob (mixture of earth and straw).

Headland:
Elevated bulk of land, overlooking a landscape.

Illusionist:
Artist who produces illusion effects. He outwits the audience with his tricks, and they think they are seeing magic.

Learned:
Extremely cultivated person, who knows a lot about one or several fields.

Leisurely:
When something is extremely pleasant, enjoyable.

Limestone:
Limestone is mostly made of calcium.

Minister of Foreign Affairs:
In charge of organising exchanges between France and foreign countries. Organises his country's foreign policy.

Nursery:
Place where children are looked after, day and night.

Paddle steamer:
It is a steam boat. It sails forward thanks to its big paddled wheels.

Pleasure homes:
These are very pleasant homes that are lovely to live in.

Prosperity:
Extremely favourable situation for a person or country, mostly from a financial aspect.

Resin:
Chemical substances used to make plastic.

Salamander:
Animal that looks like a lizard. Legend has it that they do not fear fire.

Scenography:
The art of making and placing stage décor for shows.

Sumptuous:
Luxurious. Beauty that shows a great deal of wealth.

Symmetry:
Items are symmetrical when their shape is identical on either side of a central point or axis. This is known as the symmetry axis.

Treasurer:
Person in charge of managing a country's money.

Yew:
Small evergreen tree. Belongs to the conifer family (pine trees).

Diving suit

ANSWERS

Pages 12-13:
Michel de MONTAIGNE and François RABELAIS

Page 17:

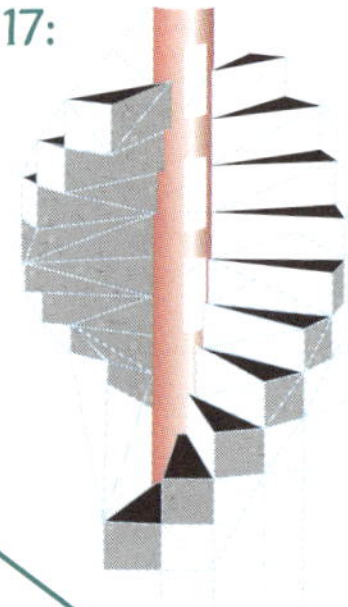

Page 19:
Between 10 °C and 15 °C all year round.

Page 20:
In the middle.

Page 21:

Page 27:

Page 29: 5-The military tank

Page 31:
Entrance E will allow you to reach the centre without coming across any rabbits.

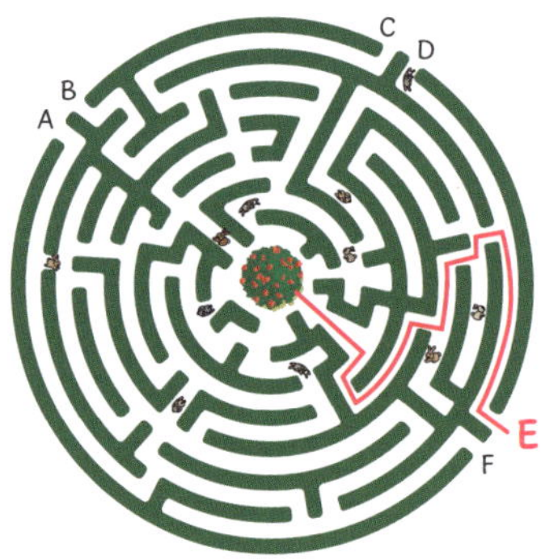

Page 32:

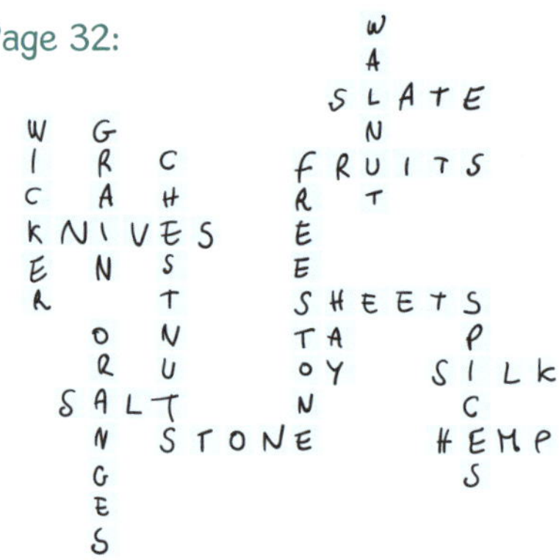

Page 35 :

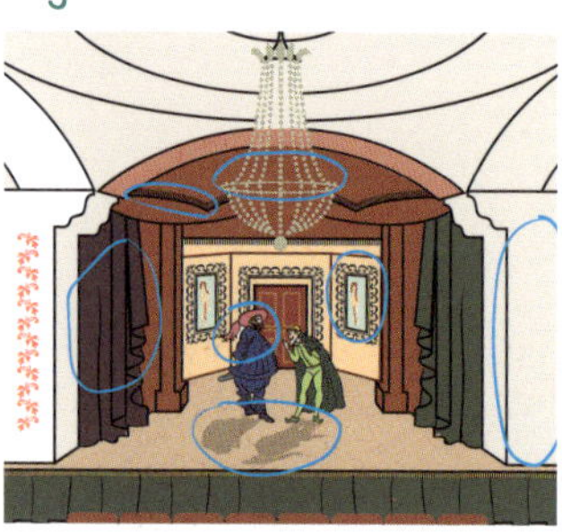

Page 36:
I dug a tunnel in the Western wall.

Page 37:
Picture A corresponds to Louise's throw.

Page 40:
B-5; C-6; D-3; E-2; F-1
The A-4 match is impossible.

Page 43:

Page 44 :
OH, IT'S JUST A SIMPLE GUEST ROOM!

Page 45 :

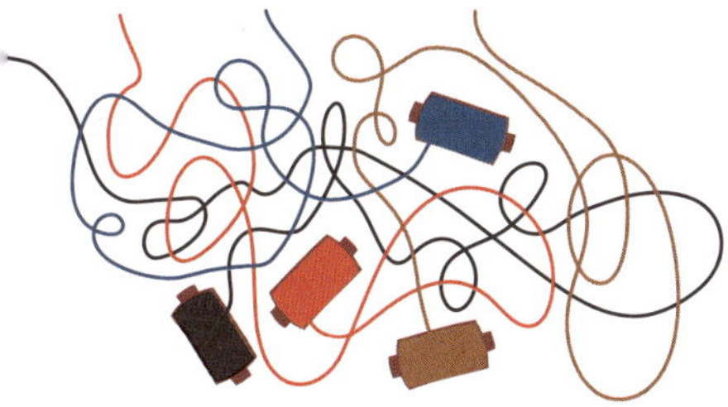

Page 47:

There are 7 ermines and 5 salamanders.

Page 49:

Ricky of the Tuft

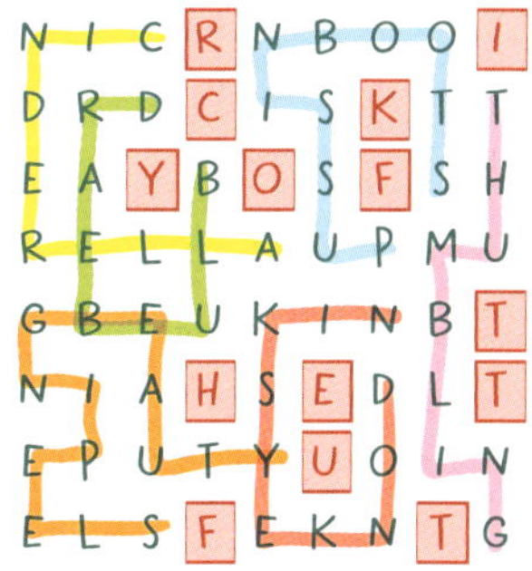

Page 51 :

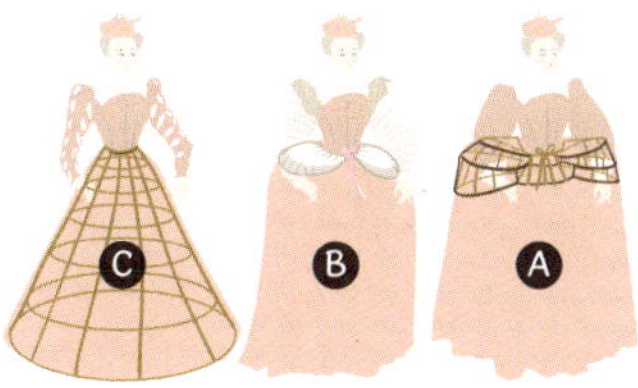

Page 54:

When he was a baby, the giant Pantagruel drank the milk of ***46x100= 4,600 cows!***

Page 53:

It is a barrel.

Page 55:

Page 57:

● - U; ★ - T; ♦ - A

Page 59:

1-A; 2-E; 3-B;
4-C; 5-F
Detail D was not taken from this part of the hanging.

Page 61:

The Dukes' château stands out with its **two very different styles.**
Outside, a formidable fortress protected by deep moats, and defended by ramparts and seven large turrets made of granite.
In total, the wall walk runs for 1,600 feet.

Inside, the Dukes' elegant residence comes as a contrast with the white tuffeau stone. The Renaissance style had just started to appear.

Authors: Stéphanie and Hugues Bioret, Julie Godefroy
Illustrators: Julie Godefroy and Stéphanie Bioret

Acknowledgements: Sarah Mousson; Mr Bastard-Musée du Compagnonnage in Tours; château de Langeais; Constance de Vivraye (château de Cheverny); Isaure de Sainte Marie (château de Troussay); Sameh Halaili (château de Chenonceau); château d'Ussé; Guy Bioret; Paula Meunier

Contact: tel. +33 (0)6 13 54 19 80
bonhommedechemin@orange.fr
www.bonhommedechemin.fr

In compliance with law no49956 from 16 July 1949 regarding publications for children

ISBN: 979-10-92714-25-8

Imprimerie Graphitilt (79) - Printed on PEFC paper
Printing completed in February 2020
Legal registration: March 2018

Despite all the care put into the design and content of this book, it is still subject to change. Please feel free to send us your comments. Suggestions are also welcome.

PEFC
10-32-3010
Certifié PEFC

IMPRIM'VERT®

Photo credits:

Hugues Bioret: *p.21: garden and park in Cheverny; p.61: sculpture of Anne of Brittany; p.24: château in Chaumont; p.38: ceiling in Chambord; p.56: Fontevraud royal abbey, recumbent statues of Eleanor of Aquitaine and Henry II in Fontevraud; back cover: Medici gallery in Chenonceaux*

Bernard and Nicole Boué: *p.36: view of the royal city of Loches; p43: château in Villandry*

©Christophe Apatie: *p.39: château in Troussay*

J.B ©Rabouan: *p45: château in Langeais*

© Wikipédia: *p.6: battle of Azincourt, miniature drawn from the Abrégé de la Chronique by Enguerrand de Monstrelet, 15th century, Paris, BnF, department of Manuscripts; p.11: tapestry by Velvet; p.12: The Birth of Venus, Sandro Botticelli; p.13: Mona Lisa, Leonardo da Vinci; p.22: emblem of Louis XII on the Hotel de Bourgtheroulde in Rouen;* p.33: *view of the Loire Christophe Finot,* CC BY-SA 3.0; the Partheno Athens, Steve Swayne, CC BY 2.0; Beijing, China by Philip Larson, CC BY-SA 2.0, Victoria Falls 35-own work, CC BY-SA 3.0; *p.35: château in Valençay; p.39: Amboise room at the château in Montpoupon; p.38. rose window in Saint-Gatien cathedral in Tours - ©Guillaume Piolle; p.39: petrifying Savonnières grottos - Duch.seb - Own work, CC BY-SA 3.0;* p40: Lepeltier Ludovic, CC BY-SA 3.0, Tours; *p48: Sleeping Beauty by Gustave Doré;* p.53: Chinon-By Zwarck-own work, CC BY-SA 3.0; *p.54: engraving by Gustave Doré of Chapter IV of Pantagruel, Garnier Frères editions, 1873; p.61: château of the Dukes of Brittany; back cover: Chambord*

© Fotolia: *p.3: Saumur and its château ©graphlight; p.7: Chenonceau engraving © Erica Guilane-Nachez; p.8: Nantes city centre ©photlook; p.9: the portcullis ©tlandry; p.10: Doge's palace ©pfeifferv; p.11: Chambord staircase ©Fabio Lotti; p.17: château in Chambord, North-West façade ©Pascal Ledard; p.25: grass ©Winyu garden; p.27: Amboise ©bannkie; p.29: Clos Lucé ©jebouc59; p.32: Loire landscape ©laurine45; p.38: the Loire and the Saint Martin basilica in Tours ©LEDAY L; p.39: Stag in the forest ©shocky; p47: Azay-le-Rideau, Loire château ©aterrom; p49: château in Ussé ©PHB.cz; p.52: ©wjarek; p.55: château in Saumur ©PHB.cz; p.59: château in Angers ©aterrom*

Pixabay: *p.5: château in Chaumont; p.18: château in Chambord; p.21: Cheverny estate; p.28: parachute, car hand-glider, helicopter, tank; p.33: Tajín in Mexico, Angkor Wat temple; p.38: Saint-Gatien cathedral in Tours; p.39: château in Sully-sur-Loire; p.52: Chinon*